Practical
Healthy Eating

p^3

This is a P³ Book
First published in 2003

P³
Queen Street House
4 Queen Street
Bath BA1 1HE, UK

ISBN: 1-40540-922-3

Printed in China

NOTE

This book uses metric and imperial measurements. Follow the same
units of measurement throughout; do not mix metric and imperial.
All spoon measurements are level: teaspoons are assumed to be 5 ml,
and tablespoons are assumed to be 15 ml. Unless otherwise stated,
eggs and individual vegetables such as potatoes are medium,
and pepper is freshly ground black pepper.

The nutritional information provided for each recipe is per serving or per person.
Optional ingredients, variations, or serving suggestions have
not been included in the calculations. The times given for each recipe are an approximate
guide only because the preparation times may differ according to the techniques used by
different people and the cooking times may vary as a result of the type of oven used.

Recipes using raw or very lightly cooked eggs should be
avoided by children, the elderly, pregnant women, convalescents,
and anyone suffering from an illness.

Contents

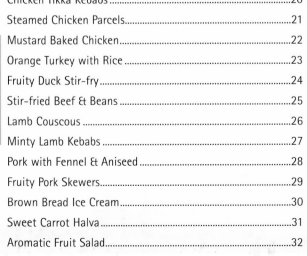

Introduction

Many of us have taken on board the message that what we eat impacts significantly on our health. However, it is easy to become bewildered by the complexities and contradictions in the advice on different foods and dietary regimes that we now face on a daily basis. This book offers a refreshing and inspirational approach to healthy eating based on sound nutritional principles and offers a range of easy-to-prepare yet imaginative recipes. The exciting flavours and textures in these dishes will serve as an antidote to the perceived view that a healthy diet is restrictive. This is food that you can really enjoy while improving your health.

Healthy eating guidelines

In order for your body to maintain itself in good working order, it needs to have a regular and balanced supply of nutrients. This means making the right choice of foods day by day, and nutritionists have developed a way of helping us to make that choice without having to grapple with detailed nutritional data. They have identified the basic food types and divided them into five separate groups. These groups are shown here, with the group we need the most listed first, reducing to those we need least listed last.

Bread, cereals, pasta, noodles, rice and potatoes

These foods are rich in carbohydrates, which provide the body with energy, and are low in fat. They contain B vitamins, selenium, calcium and iron as well as fibre. Up to a third of your daily food intake should be chosen from this group.

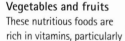

Vegetables and fruits

These nutritious foods are rich in vitamins, particularly A, C and E, known as antioxidants, and minerals such as calcium, potassium, magnesium and iron. They are good sources of fibre and are virtually fat-free. You can eat as many as you like of these, and most health organizations recommend eating at least five portions in total a day.

Meat, poultry, fish, beans, nuts, seeds and eggs

These foods are our main source of protein, essential for maintaining the body's functions. Meat, poultry and fish are rich in B vitamins and minerals such as iron, zinc and magnesium, but they also contain varying amounts of saturated and unsaturated fat.

Milk, cheese and yogurt

Dairy foods offer good sources of calcium, provide protein, and contain vitamins A, D and B6 (riboflavin), but they are also high in saturated fats, so your consumption needs to be limited. Choosing lower-fat varieties of these foods will help in this way.

Fats and sugars These foods are essential to a healthy diet but they are only needed in small quantities, so they should make up the smallest proportion of your daily food intake. It is preferable to eat more unsaturated fats than saturated fats. Unsaturated fats are found in olive oil and other vegetable oils, oily fish and fish oils, avocados, nuts and seeds.

Healthy ingredients and options

While the carbohydrate-rich foods are the mainstay of a healthy diet, we need to be wary of falling into the trap of eating them with saturated fats and sugars – for instance, breakfast cereals with sugar and milk, pasta with creamy sauces, bread spread with butter and jam, or potatoes in

the form of chips, deep-fried in oil. There are many other ways to enjoy carbohydrates without counteracting their beneficial effects. For extra benefits, opting for wholemeal or whole-grain varieties of bread, rice, pasta and breakfast cereals will maximise your intake of dietary fibre and vitamins.

Variety is the key to getting the most from vegetables and fruits in your diet, in terms of both the different nutrients they have and their fibre content, in addition to taste and texture. Bananas, for instance, are rich in potassium, which can help to regulate blood pressure, and citrus fruits are high in fibre and vitamin C. Spinach, carrots and peppers offer beta-carotene, which the body converts into vitamin A. Some studies have found that lycopene, which gives tomatoes their bright red colouring, can help to reduce the risk of prostate cancer in men, and possibly cervical cancer in women. It appears that canned or otherwise processed tomatoes are even more beneficial than the fresh variety.

You can avoid loss of vitamins from vegetables and fruits by taking a few simple steps in their preparation. Avoid peeling them where possible, avoid letting them stand in water before cooking, and avoid overcooking them. Where possible, steam or bake them, or simmer in a minimal amount of water.

Your choice of protein source has an important part to play in maintaining a healthy diet. Skinless turkey and chicken are relatively low in fat, particularly saturated fats, although the brown meat is fattier than the white. Lean cuts of pork are surprisingly low in fat – more so than beef or lamb. While white fish is low in fat, oily fish such as salmon, tuna, mackerel, herrings, sardines and anchovies contains omega-3 fatty acids, which are thought to be protective against heart disease and strokes, and may be helpful for those suffering from psoriasis or arthritis. Canned varieties are no less beneficial in this respect. Tofu is a particularly healthy protein source: it is low in saturated fat and cholesterol and contains protective antioxidants. Dried beans, peas and lentils are another good, low-fat source of protein, but they are best served with whole-grain rice and plant foods to provide the correct balance of nutrients, particularly within a vegetarian diet. Nuts are high in fat, but it is mostly of the unsaturated kind, which, rather than raising blood cholesterol levels, may even help to reduce them. Hazelnuts, walnuts and almonds are good choices.

Fatty foods are seductive because the fats and oils they contain are phenomenal flavour-boosters. However, other healthier ingredients can be used in place of fats to contribute to the taste of dishes, such as fresh herbs, including garlic and fresh root ginger, dried herbs, spices, tomato purée, olives, capers, reduced-salt soy sauce, Worcestershire sauce, Tabasco sauce, stock, vegetable and fruit juices and wine.

Healthy cooking methods

Once you have chosen the right foods for a healthy, balanced diet, it is vital to follow through with a healthy approach to cooking them. Steaming requires no additional fat and retains nutrients and flavour, while grilling, barbecuing or griddling (using a dry cast-iron or aluminium ridged grill pan on the hob) seals in flavour with little or no need for fat. Rapidly stir-frying foods in a wok in a minimal amount of oil is also a relatively healthy cooking method, and again maximises the taste and texture of ingredients. Microwaving is also a fat-free cooking method. Using a heavy-based, non-stick frying pan, you can dry-fry minced meat or bacon, thereby releasing its own fat, which can then be drained away. Use a proprietary oil spray for pan-frying, or alternatively, try 'sautéeing' vegetables without any additional fat in a covered pan, where they will cook in their own juices.

KEY		
	Simplicity level 1–3 (1 easiest, 3 slightly harder)	
	Preparation time	
	Cooking time	

Bacon, Bean & Garlic Soup

This is a mouthwatering and healthy vegetable, bean and bacon soup, which you can cook in a microwave oven. Serve it with wholemeal bread.

NUTRITIONAL INFORMATION

Calories 261   Sugars 5g
Protein . . . . .23g   Fat 8g
Carbohydrate . . .25g   Saturates 2g

🔥 5 mins   🕐 20 mins

SERVES 4

I N G R E D I E N T S

225 g/8 oz lean smoked back bacon slices

1 carrot, thinly sliced

1 celery stick, thinly sliced

1 onion, chopped

1 tbsp oil

3 garlic cloves, sliced

700 ml/1¼ pints hot vegetable stock

200 g/7 oz canned chopped tomatoes

1 tbsp chopped fresh thyme

about 400 g/14 oz canned cannellini
      beans, drained

1 tbsp tomato purée

salt and pepper

grated Cheddar cheese, to garnish

COOK'S TIP

For a more substantial soup, add 60 g/2¼ oz small pasta shapes or short lengths of spaghetti when you add the stock and tomatoes. You will also need to add an extra 150 ml/5 fl oz vegetable stock.

1 Chop 2 slices of the bacon and place in a microwave-proof bowl. Microwave on High power for 3–4 minutes until the fat runs out and the bacon is well cooked. Stir the bacon halfway through cooking to separate the pieces. Transfer to a plate lined with kitchen paper and leave to cool. When cool, the bacon pieces should be crisp and dry. Place the carrot, celery, onion and oil in a microwave-proof bowl. Cover and cook on High power for 4 minutes.

2 Chop the remaining bacon and add to the bowl with the garlic. Cover and cook on High power for 2 minutes.

3 Add the stock, the contents of the can of tomatoes, the thyme, beans and tomato purée. Cover and cook on High power for 8 minutes, stirring halfway through. Season to taste. Ladle the soup into warmed bowls and sprinkle with the crisp bacon and grated cheese.

Red Lentil Soup with Yogurt

This tasty red lentil soup flavoured with chopped coriander is an easy microwave dish. The yogurt adds a light piquancy to the soup.

NUTRITIONAL INFORMATION

Calories 280   Sugars 6g
Protein . . . . .17g   Fat 7g
Carbohydrate . . .40g   Saturates 4g

5 mins   30 mins

SERVES 4

I N G R E D I E N T S

2 tbsp butter

1 onion, finely chopped

1 celery stick, finely chopped

1 large carrot, grated

1 bay leaf

225 g/8 oz red lentils

1.2 litres/2 pints hot vegetable stock or chicken stock

2 tbsp chopped fresh coriander

4 tbsp low-fat natural yogurt

salt and pepper

sprigs of fresh coriander, to garnish

1 Place the butter, onion and celery in a microwave-proof bowl. Cover and microwave on High power for 3 minutes.

2 Add the carrot, bay leaf and lentils. Pour in the stock. Cover and cook on High power for 15 minutes, stirring halfway through.

3 Remove the bowl from the microwave oven, cover, and stand for 5 minutes.

4 Remove and discard the bay leaf, then process, in batches, in a food processor until smooth. Alternatively, press the soup through a sieve.

5 Pour the soup into a clean bowl. Season with salt and pepper to taste and stir in the coriander. Cover and microwave on High power for 4–5 minutes until the soup is piping hot.

6 Serve in warmed soup bowls. Add 1 tablespoon of yogurt to each serving and garnish with small sprigs of fresh coriander.

COOK'S TIP

For an extra creamy soup, try using low-fat crème fraîche or soured cream instead of yogurt.

Crudités with Shrimp Sauce

In this delicious yet low-fat recipe, fruit and vegetable crudités are served with a spicy, garlicky shrimp sauce.

NUTRITIONAL INFORMATION

Calories	85	Sugars	........11g
Protein	.........7g	Fat	..........1g
Carbohydrate	...12g	Saturates	.....0.2g

12¼ hrs   0 mins

SERVES 4

INGREDIENTS

about 750 g/1 lb 10 oz prepared
  raw fruit and vegetables, such
  as broccoli, cauliflower, apple,
  pineapple, cucumber, celery,
  peppers and mushrooms

SAUCE

60 g/2¼ oz dried shrimps

1-cm/½-inch cube shrimp paste

3 garlic cloves, crushed

4 red chillies, deseeded and chopped

6 stems fresh coriander, coarsely chopped

juice of 2 limes

fish sauce, to taste

brown sugar, to taste

1 To make the sauce, put the dried shrimps in a bowl of warm water and soak for 10 minutes, then drain.

2 Place the shrimp paste, drained shrimps, garlic, chillies and coriander in a food processor or blender and process until well chopped but not smooth.

3 Turn the sauce mixture into a bowl and add the lime juice, mixing well.

4 Add fish sauce and brown sugar to taste, then mix well.

5 Cover the bowl tightly and chill the sauce in the refrigerator for at least 12 hours, or overnight.

6 To serve, arrange the fruit and vegetables attractively on a large serving plate. Place the prepared sauce in the centre for dipping.

COOK'S TIP

Hard-boiled quail's eggs can be added to this traditional fruit and vegetable platter to create a dish for a special occasion.

Vegetables with Sesame Dip

This tasty dip is great for livening up simply cooked vegetables. Varying the vegetables according to the season adds interest to the dish.

NUTRITIONAL INFORMATION	
Calories 126	Sugars 7g
Protein 11g	Fat 6g
Carbohydrate 8g	Saturates 1g

 5 mins — 20 mins

SERVES 4

I N G R E D I E N T S

225 g/8 oz small broccoli florets

225 g/8 oz small cauliflower florets

225 g/8 oz asparagus, sliced into 5-cm/
2-inch lengths

2 small red onions, cut into quarters

1 tbsp lime juice

2 tsp toasted sesame seeds

1 tbsp chopped fresh chives, to garnish

HOT SESAME &
GARLIC DIP

1 tsp sunflower oil

2 garlic cloves, crushed

½–1 tsp chilli powder

2 tsp tahini (sesame seed paste)

150 g/5½ oz low-fat natural fromage frais

2 tbsp chopped fresh chives

salt and pepper

1 Line the bottom of a steamer with baking paper and arrange the broccoli florets, cauliflower florets, asparagus, and onion pieces on top.

2 Bring a wok or large saucepan of water to the boil, and place the steamer on top. Sprinkle the vegetables with lime juice and steam them for 10 minutes or until they are just tender.

3 To make the Hot Sesame & Garlic Dip, heat the oil in a small, non-stick saucepan, add the garlic, chilli powder, and seasoning to taste, and cook gently for 2–3 minutes until the garlic is soft.

4 Remove the pan from the heat and stir in the tahini and fromage frais. Return the pan to the heat and cook gently for 1–2 minutes without bringing to the boil. Stir in the chives.

5 Remove the vegetables from the steamer and place on a warmed serving platter. Sprinkle them with the sesame seeds and garnish with chopped chives. Serve with the Hot Sesame & Garlic Dip.

Mixed Bean & Apple Salad

Use any mixture of beans you have to hand in this recipe, but the wider the variety, the more colourful the salad.

NUTRITIONAL INFORMATION

Calories	183	Sugars	.........8g
Protein	.........6g	Fat	...........7g
Carbohydrate	...26g	Saturates	.......1g

20 mins   20 mins

SERVES 4

INGREDIENTS

225 g/8 oz new potatoes, scrubbed and cut into quarters

225 g/8 oz mixed canned beans, such as red kidney beans, borlotti beans and small cannellini beans, drained and rinsed

1 red eating apple, diced and tossed in 1 tbsp lemon juice

1 yellow pepper, deseeded and diced

1 shallot, sliced

½ fennel bulb, sliced

oakleaf lettuce leaves

DRESSING

1 tbsp red wine vinegar

2 tbsp olive oil

1½ tsp mild yellow mustard

1 garlic clove, crushed

2 tsp chopped fresh thyme

1 Cook the potatoes in a saucepan of boiling water for 15 minutes until tender. Drain and transfer to a large bowl.

2 Add the mixed beans to the potatoes, with the diced apple, yellow pepper and sliced shallot and fennel. Mix together thoroughly, taking care not to break up the cooked potatoes.

3 To make the dressing, whisk all the dressing ingredients together until thoroughly combined, then pour it over the potato salad.

4 Line a serving plate or salad bowl with the oakleaf lettuce leaves and spoon the potato mixture into the centre. Serve the salad immediately.

VARIATION

Use Dijon or whole-grain mustard in place of mild yellow mustard for a different flavour.

Broccoli & Almond Salad

This is a colourful, crunchy salad with a delicious dressing. It is better left overnight if possible for the flavours to mingle.

NUTRITIONAL INFORMATION	
Calories 181	Sugars 7g
Protein 9g	Fat 12g
Carbohydrate 9g	Saturates 2g

4½ hrs   10 mins

SERVES 4

I N G R E D I E N T S

450 g/1 lb small broccoli florets

50 g/1¾ oz baby corn cobs, halved lengthways

1 red pepper, deseeded and cut into thin strips

50 g/1¾ oz blanched almonds

D R E S S I N G

1 tbsp sesame seeds

1 tbsp ground nut oil

2 garlic cloves, crushed

2 tbsp light soy sauce

1 tbsp clear honey

2 tsp lemon juice

pepper

lemon zest, to garnish (optional)

1 Blanch the broccoli and baby corn cobs in boiling water for 5 minutes. Drain well, rinse and drain again.

2 Transfer the broccoli and baby corn cobs to a large mixing bowl and add the red pepper and almonds.

3 To make the dressing, heat a wok and add the sesame seeds. Dry-fry, stirring constantly, for about 1 minute, or until the sesame seeds are lightly browned and are giving off a delicious aroma.

4 Mix the oil, garlic, soy sauce, honey, lemon juice and pepper in a bowl. Add the sesame seeds and mix well.

5 Pour the dressing over the salad, cover with clingfilm and set aside in the refrigerator for a minimum of 4 hours and preferably overnight.

6 Garnish the salad with lemon zest, if using, and serve.

COOK'S TIP
Take care when browning the sesame seeds because they will quickly burn. Dry-fry over a low heat and stir constantly.

Rice with Fruit & Nuts

This spicy and filling rice dish includes fruits for a refreshing flavour and toasted nuts for a crunchy texture.

NUTRITIONAL INFORMATION

Calories	423	Sugars	........19g
Protein	........10g	Fat	..........17g
Carbohydrate	...62g	Saturates	.......2g

🍚 20 mins   🕐 1 hr

SERVES 6

INGREDIENTS

4 tbsp ghee or vegetable oil

1 large onion, chopped

2 garlic cloves, crushed

2.5-cm/1-inch piece of fresh root ginger, chopped

1 tsp chilli powder

1 tsp cumin seeds

1 tbsp mild or medium curry powder or paste

300 g/10½ oz brown rice

850 ml/1½ pints boiling vegetable stock

400 g/14 oz canned chopped tomatoes

175 g/6 oz ready-to-eat dried apricots or peaches, cut into slivers

1 red pepper, deseeded and diced

85 g/3 oz frozen peas

1–2 small, slightly green bananas

55–85 g/2–3 oz toasted nuts, such as almonds, cashew nuts, and hazelnuts or pine kernels

salt and pepper

sprigs of fresh coriander, to garnish

1 Heat the ghee or oil in a large saucepan. Add the onion and cook over a low heat for 3 minutes. Stir in the garlic, ginger, spices, and rice and cook gently, stirring constantly, for 2 minutes until the rice is coated in the spiced oil.

2 Pour in the boiling stock, add the chopped tomatoes, and season with salt and pepper to taste. Bring to the boil, then lower the heat, cover, and simmer gently for 40 minutes, or until the rice is almost cooked and most of the liquid has been absorbed.

3 Add the slivered apricots or peaches, diced red pepper, and peas. Cover and continue cooking for 10 minutes. Remove from the heat and set aside for 5 minutes without uncovering.

4 Peel and slice the bananas. Uncover the rice mixture and fork through thoroughly to mix the ingredients and fluff up the rice. Add the sliced bananas and toasted nuts and toss the mixture lightly. Transfer to a warmed serving platter and garnish with sprigs of fresh coriander. Serve immediately.

Spinach & Nut Pilau

Fragrant basmati rice is cooked with porcini mushrooms, spinach and pistachio nuts in this easy microwave recipe.

NUTRITIONAL INFORMATION	
Calories 403	Sugars 7g
Protein 10g	Fat 15g
Carbohydrate ...62g	Saturates 2g

🍲 55 mins   🕐 15–20 mins

SERVES 4

I N G R E D I E N T S

10 g/¼ oz dried porcini mushrooms

300 ml/10 fl oz hot water

1 onion, chopped

1 garlic clove, crushed

1 tsp grated root ginger

½ fresh green chilli, deseeded and chopped

2 tbsp oil

225 g/8 oz basmati rice

1 large carrot, grated

175 ml/6 fl oz vegetable stock

½ tsp ground cinnamon

4 cloves

½ tsp saffron strands

225 g/8 oz fresh spinach, long stalks removed

60 g/2¼ oz pistachio nuts

1 tbsp chopped fresh coriander

salt and pepper

sprigs of fresh coriander, to garnish

1 Place the porcini mushrooms in a small bowl. Pour over the hot water and leave to soak for 30 minutes.

2 Place the onion, garlic, ginger, chilli and oil in a microwave-proof bowl. Cover and microwave on High power for 2 minutes. Rinse the rice, then stir it into the bowl, together with the carrot. Cover and cook on High power for 1 minute.

3 Strain and coarsely chop the mushrooms. Add enough mushroom soaking liquid to the stock to make 425 ml/15 fl oz. Pour on to the rice.

4 Stir in the mushrooms, cinnamon, cloves, saffron, and ½ teaspoon salt. Cover and cook on High power for 10 minutes, stirring once. Leave the mixture to stand, covered, for 10 minutes.

5 Place the spinach in another microwave-proof bowl. Cover and cook on High power for 3½ minutes, stirring once. Drain well and chop the spinach coarsely.

6 Stir the spinach, pistachio nuts, and chopped coriander into the rice. Season to taste with salt and pepper and garnish with sprigs of fresh coriander. Serve immediately.

Gorgonzola & Pumpkin Pizza

Blue Gorgonzola cheese and juicy pears make a good combination in this colourful pizza. The wholemeal base adds a nutty flavour and texture.

NUTRITIONAL INFORMATION

Calories	470	Sugars	.........5g
Protein	........17g	Fat	..........15g
Carbohydrate	...72g	Saturates	.......6g

 1¼ hrs ⏱ 35 mins

SERVES 4

INGREDIENTS

PIZZA BASE

2 tsp dried yeast

1 tsp sugar

225 ml/8 fl oz lukewarm water

175 g/6 oz wholemeal plain flour

175 g/6 oz white bread flour

1 tsp salt

1 tbsp olive oil, plus extra for greasing

TOPPING

450 g/1 lb pumpkin or squash, peeled and cubed

1 tbsp olive oil

1 pear, cored, peeled, and sliced

100 g/3½ oz Gorgonzola cheese, crumbled

fresh rosemary, to garnish

1 To make the dough, place the yeast and sugar in a jug and mix with 4 tablespoons of the lukewarm water. Leave the yeast mixture to stand in a warm place for 15 minutes or until foamy.

2 Combine both of the flours with the salt and make a well in the centre. Add the oil, the yeast mixture and the remaining water. Using a wooden spoon, mix to form a dough.

3 Turn the dough out on to a floured work surface and then knead for 4–5 minutes or until smooth.

4 Return the dough to the bowl, cover with an oiled sheet of clingfilm and leave to rise for 30 minutes or until doubled in size.

5 Remove the dough from the bowl. Knead the dough for 2 minutes. Using a rolling pin, roll out the dough to form a long oval shape, then place it on an oiled baking sheet, pushing out the edges until even. The dough should be no more than 5 mm/¼ inch thick because it will rise during cooking.

6 To make the topping, place the pumpkin in a shallow roasting tin. Drizzle with the olive oil and cook under a preheated grill for 20 minutes or until soft and lightly golden.

7 Top the dough with the pumpkin and pear, brushing with the oil from the pan. Scatter over the Gorgonzola. Bake in a preheated oven, 200°C/400°F/Gas Mark 6, for about 15 minutes or until the base is golden. Garnish with rosemary and serve.

Tofu with Mushrooms

Chinese mushrooms are available from Chinese food shops and health food shops and add a unique flavour to Oriental dishes.

NUTRITIONAL INFORMATION

Calories	218	Sugars	.........1g
Protein	........12g	Fat	..........14g
Carbohydrate	...13g	Saturates	.......2g

15 mins   15 mins

SERVES 4

INGREDIENTS

25 g/1 oz dried Chinese mushrooms

450 g/1 lb firm tofu

4 tbsp cornflour

oil, for deep-frying

2 garlic cloves, finely chopped

2 tsp grated fresh root ginger

100 g/3½ oz frozen or fresh peas

1 Place the Chinese mushrooms in a large heatproof bowl. Pour in enough boiling water to cover and leave to stand for about 10 minutes.

2 Meanwhile, using a sharp knife, cut the tofu into bite-sized cubes.

3 Place the cornflour in a large bowl. Add the tofu to the bowl and toss in the cornflour until evenly coated.

4 Heat the oil for deep-frying in a large preheated wok.

5 Add the cubes of tofu to the wok and then deep-fry them, in batches, for about 2–3 minutes or until they are golden and crispy. Remove the cooked tofu with a slotted spoon and then drain on kitchen paper.

6 Drain off all but 2 tablespoons of oil from the wok. Add the garlic, ginger and Chinese mushrooms to the wok and cook for 2–3 minutes.

7 Return the cooked tofu to the wok and add the peas. Heat through for 1 minute then serve hot.

COOK'S TIP

Chinese dried mushrooms add flavour and a distinctive aroma. They are sold dried in packets, and they can be expensive, but only a few are needed per dish and they store indefinitely. If they are unavailable, use open-cap mushrooms instead.

Yucatan Fish

Herbs, onion, green pepper and pumpkin seeds are used to flavour this baked fish, which is first marinated in lime juice.

NUTRITIONAL INFORMATION

Calories 248   Sugars 2g
Protein . . . . .33g   Fat 11g
Carbohydrate . . . .3g   Saturates 1g

🧊 40 mins   🕒 35 mins

SERVES 4

I N G R E D I E N T S

4 cod cutlets or steaks, or hake cutlets
   (about 175 g/6 oz each)

2 tbsp lime juice

1 green pepper

1 tbsp olive oil

1 onion, finely chopped

1–2 garlic cloves, crushed

40 g/1½ oz green pumpkin seeds

grated rind of ½ lime

1 tbsp chopped fresh coriander or parsley

1 tbsp chopped fresh mixed herbs

60 g/2¼ oz button mushrooms,
   thinly sliced

2–3 tbsp fresh orange juice or
   white wine

salt and pepper

T O   G A R N I S H

lime wedges

fresh mixed herbs

1 Wipe the fish, place in a shallow, non-metallic, ovenproof dish, and pour over the lime juice. Turn the fish in the juice, season with salt and pepper, cover, and leave to stand in a cool place for 15–30 minutes.

2 Halve the green pepper, remove the seeds, and place under a preheated moderate grill, skin-side upwards, until the skin burns and splits. Leave to cool slightly, then peel off the skin and chop the flesh.

3 Heat the oil in a frying pan and cook the onion, garlic, green pepper and pumpkin seeds gently for a few minutes until the onion is soft.

4 Stir in the lime rind, coriander or parsley, mixed herbs, mushrooms and seasoning, and spoon over the fish.

5 Spoon or pour the orange juice or wine over the fish, cover with foil or a lid, and place in a preheated oven, 180°C/350°F/Gas Mark 4, for about 30 minutes or until the fish is just tender.

6 Remove the fish from the oven, garnish with lime wedges and fresh mixed herbs, and serve.

Fish & Yogurt Quenelles

These quenelles, made from a thick purée of fish and yogurt, can be prepared well in advance and stored in the refrigerator before poaching.

NUTRITIONAL INFORMATION	
Calories 228	Sugars 7g
Protein 39g	Fat 2g
Carbohydrate ...14g	Saturates 1g

45 mins   15 mins

SERVES 4

I N G R E D I E N T S

750 g/1 lb 10 oz white fish fillets, such as cod, coley or whiting, skinned

2 small egg whites

½ tsp ground coriander

1 tsp ground mace

150 ml/5 fl oz low-fat natural yogurt

1 small onion, sliced

salt and pepper

mixture of boiled basmati rice and wild rice, to serve

S A U C E

1 bunch of watercress, trimmed

300 ml/10 fl oz chicken stock

2 tbsp cornflour

150 ml/5 fl oz low-fat natural yogurt

2 tbsp low-fat crème fraîche

1 Cut the fish into pieces and process it in a food processor for 30 seconds. Add the egg whites and process for another 30 seconds to a stiff paste. Add the coriander, mace, yogurt and seasoning, and process until smooth. Cover and chill for at least 30 minutes.

2 Spoon the mixture into a piping bag, and pipe into sausage shapes about 10 cm/4 inches long. Alternatively, take rounded dessertspoons of the mixture and shape into ovals using 2 spoons.

3 Bring about 5 cm/2 inches of water to the boil in a frying pan and add the onion. Lower the quenelles into the water, using a fish slice or spoon. Cover the pan and poach for 8 minutes, turning once. Remove with a slotted spoon and drain.

4 Chop the watercress, reserving a few sprigs for the garnish. Process the remainder with the stock, then pour into a small saucepan. Stir the cornflour into the yogurt, and then pour into the pan. Bring to the boil, stirring. Stir in the crème fraîche, season with salt and pepper, and remove from the heat. Garnish with the reserved watercress, and serve with cooked basmati and wild rice.

Balti Cod & Red Lentils

The aniseed in this recipe gives a very delicate aroma to the fish and really enhances the flavour. Serve with warm wholemeal bread.

NUTRITIONAL INFORMATION

Calories	236	Sugars 3g
Protein	........29g	Fat 7g
Carbohydrate	...15g	Saturates 1g

 5 mins 1 hr

SERVES 4

INGREDIENTS

2 tbsp oil

¼ tsp ground asafoetida (optional)

1 tbsp crushed aniseed

1 tsp ground ginger

1 tsp chilli powder

¼ tsp ground turmeric

225 g/8 oz split red lentils

1 tsp salt

500 g/1 lb 2 oz cod, skinned, filleted and cut into 2.5-cm/1-inch cubes

1 fresh red chilli, chopped

3 tbsp low-fat natural yogurt

2 tbsp chopped fresh coriander

warm wholemeal bread, to serve

 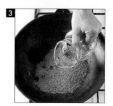 

COOK'S TIP

Ground asafoetida is easier to use than the type that comes in a block. It should only be used in small quantities. Do not be put off by the smell, which is very pungent.

1 Heat the oil in a Balti pan or wok, add the asafoetida, if using, and cook for about 10 seconds to burn off the smell of the asafoetida.

2 Add the aniseed, ginger, chilli powder and turmeric and cook for 30 seconds.

3 Wash the lentils thoroughly, then add to the pan with the salt and enough water to cover.

4 Bring to the boil, then simmer gently for 45 minutes until the lentils are soft but not mushy.

5 Add the cod pieces and chopped red chilli, bring to the boil, and simmer for another 10 minutes.

6 Stir the yogurt and fresh coriander into the fish mixture and serve with warm wholemeal bread.

Salmon Fillet with Herbs

This is a great party dish. The salmon is cooked with fennel, and the combination of the herbs and barbecue flavour makes it truly irresistible.

NUTRITIONAL INFORMATION

Calories	...... .507	Sugars	...... .0.4g
Protein	...... .46g	Fat	...... .35g
Carbohydrate	...0.5g	Saturates	...... .6g

 5 mins   🕐 30 mins

SERVES 4

I N G R E D I E N T S

½ large bunch dried thyme

5 fresh rosemary branches, 15–20 cm/
  6–8 inches long

8 bay leaves

1 kg/2 lb 4 oz salmon fillet

1 bulb fennel, cut into 8 pieces

2 tbsp lemon juice

2 tbsp olive oil

TO SERVE

crusty bread

fresh salad leaves

1 Make a base on a preheated hot barbecue with the dried thyme, rosemary branches and bay leaves, overlapping them so that they cover a slightly larger area than the salmon.

2 Carefully place the salmon on top of the herbs.

3 Arrange the fennel around the edge of the fish.

4 Combine the lemon juice and oil and brush the salmon with it.

5 Cover the salmon loosely with a piece of foil, to keep it moist.

6 Cook for about 20–30 minutes, basting frequently with the lemon juice mixture.

7 Remove the cooked salmon from the barbecue, cut it into slices, and arrange the fennel around it.

8 Serve with slices of crusty bread and fresh salad leaves.

VARIATION

Use whatever combination of herbs you may have to hand – but avoid the stronger tasting herbs, such as sage and marjoram, which are unsuitable for fish.

Chicken Tikka Kebabs

Chicken tikka is a low-fat Indian dish. Recipes vary, but you can try your own combination of spices to suit your personal taste.

NUTRITIONAL INFORMATION	
Calories 191	Sugars 8g
Protein 30g	Fat 4g
Carbohydrate 8g	Saturates 2g

2¼ hrs   15 mins

SERVES 4

INGREDIENTS

4 skinless, boneless chicken breast
  portions, about 125 g/4½ oz each

1 large ripe mango

1 tbsp lime juice

fresh coriander leaves, to garnish

MARINADE

1 garlic clove, crushed

1 tsp grated fresh root ginger

1 fresh green chilli, deseeded and
  finely chopped

6 tbsp low-fat natural yogurt

1 tbsp tomato purée

1 tsp ground cumin

1 tsp ground coriander

1 tsp ground turmeric

salt and pepper

TO SERVE

boiled white rice

lime wedges

mixed salad leaves

warmed naan bread

1 Cut the chicken into 2.5-cm/1-inch cubes and place in a shallow dish.

2 To make the marinade, combine the garlic, ginger, chilli, yogurt, tomato purée, spices and seasoning. Spoon over the chicken, cover, and chill for 2 hours.

3 Using a vegetable peeler, peel the skin from the mango. Slice down either side of the stone and cut the mango flesh into cubes. Toss in lime juice, cover, and chill until required.

4 Thread the chicken and mango pieces alternately on to 8 skewers. Place the skewers on a grill rack and brush the chicken with the yogurt marinade and the lime juice left from the mango.

5 Place under a preheated moderate grill and cook for 6–7 minutes. Turn over, brush again with the marinade and lime juice, and cook for 6–7 minutes until the juices run clear when the chicken is pierced with a sharp knife.

6 Serve the kebabs immediately on a bed of rice on a warmed platter, garnished with fresh coriander leaves and accompanied by lime wedges, mixed salad leaves and warmed naan bread.

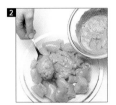

Steamed Chicken Parcels

This is a healthy recipe with a delicate Oriental flavour. Use large spinach leaves to wrap around the chicken, but make sure they are young leaves.

NUTRITIONAL INFORMATION

Calories 216	Sugars 7g	
Protein 31g	Fat 7g	
Carbohydrate 7g	Saturates 2g	

20 mins   30 mins

SERVES 4

I N G R E D I E N T S

4 lean, skinless, boneless chicken breasts

1 tsp ground lemon grass

2 spring onions, finely chopped

250 g/9 oz young carrots

250 g/9 oz young courgettes

2 sticks celery

1 tsp light soy sauce

250 g/9 oz spinach leaves

2 tsp sesame oil

salt and pepper

1 With a sharp knife, make a slit through one side of each chicken breast, to open out a large pocket.

2 Sprinkle the inside of the pocket with lemon grass, and salt and pepper. Tuck the spring onions into the pockets.

3 Trim the carrots, courgettes and celery, then cut into small matchsticks. Plunge them into a pan of boiling water for 1 minute, then drain and toss in the soy sauce.

4 Pack the mixture into the pockets in the chicken breasts and fold over firmly to enclose it. Reserve the remaining vegetables. Wash and dry the spinach leaves, then wrap the chicken breasts firmly in the leaves to enclose completely. If the leaves are too firm, steam them for a few seconds until softened and flexible.

5 Place the wrapped chicken in a steamer and then steam over rapidly boiling water for about 20–25 minutes depending on size.

6 Stir-fry any leftover vegetable sticks and spinach for 1–2 minutes in the sesame oil and serve with the chicken.

Mustard Baked Chicken

In this dish, chicken pieces are cooked in a succulent mild mustard sauce, coated in poppy seeds, and served on a bed of fresh pasta shells.

NUTRITIONAL INFORMATION

Calories	652	Sugars	.........5g
Protein	........51g	Fat	..........31g
Carbohydrate	...46g	Saturates	......12g

10 mins   35 mins

SERVES 4

I N G R E D I E N T S

8 chicken pieces, 115 g/4 oz each

4 tbsp butter, melted

4 tbsp mild mustard (see Cook's Tip)

2 tbsp lemon juice

1 tbsp brown sugar

1 tsp paprika

3 tbsp poppy seeds

400 g/14 oz dried pasta shells

1 tbsp olive oil

salt and pepper

1 Arrange the chicken pieces in a single layer in a large ovenproof dish.

2 Combine the butter, mustard, lemon juice, brown sugar, and paprika in a bowl and season with salt and pepper to taste. Brush the mixture over the upper surfaces of the chicken pieces and then bake in a preheated oven, 200°C/400°F/ Gas Mark 6, for 15 minutes.

3 Remove the dish from the oven and carefully turn over the chicken pieces. Coat the upper surfaces of the chicken with the remaining mustard mixture, sprinkle the chicken pieces with poppy seeds, and return to the oven for another 15 minutes.

4 Meanwhile, bring a large saucepan of lightly salted water to the boil. Add the pasta shells and olive oil, bring back to the boil, and cook for 8–10 minutes or until tender but still firm to the bite.

5 Drain the pasta thoroughly and arrange on a warm serving dish. Top the pasta with the chicken pieces, pour the mustard sauce over them, and serve immediately.

COOK'S TIP

Dijon mustard is most often used in cooking because it has a clean and mildly spicy flavour. German mustard has a sweet-sour taste, and Bavarian mustard is slightly sweeter. American mustard is mild and sweet.

Orange Turkey with Rice

This is a good way to use up leftover rice. Use fresh or canned sweet pink grapefruit for an interesting alternative to the orange.

NUTRITIONAL INFORMATION

Calories 337   Sugars 12g
Protein . . . . 32g   Fat 7g
Carbohydrate . . . 40g   Saturates 1g

30 mins   40 mins

SERVES 4

I N G R E D I E N T S

1 tbsp olive oil

1 medium onion, chopped

450 g/1 lb skinless lean turkey (such as fillet), cut into thin strips

300 ml/10 fl oz unsweetened orange juice

1 bay leaf

225 g/8 oz small broccoli florets

1 large courgette, diced

1 large orange

350 g/12 oz cooked brown rice

salt and pepper

tomato and onion salad, to serve

T O   G A R N I S H

25 g/1 oz stoned black olives in brine, drained and cut into quarters

shredded basil leaves

1 Heat the oil in a large frying pan and cook the onion and turkey, stirring, for 4–5 minutes until lightly browned.

2 Pour in the orange juice and add the bay leaf and seasoning. Bring to the boil and simmer for 10 minutes.

3 Meanwhile, bring a large saucepan of water to the boil and cook the broccoli florets, covered, for 2 minutes. Add the

diced courgette, then bring back to the boil. Cover and cook for another 3 minutes. Do not overcook. Drain and set aside.

4 Using a sharp knife, peel off the skin and white pith from the orange. Slice down the orange to make thin circular slices, then halve each slice.

5 Stir the broccoli, courgette, rice, and orange slices into the turkey mixture.

Gently mix together and season, then heat through for another 3–4 minutes or until the mixture is piping hot.

6 Transfer the turkey rice to warm serving plates and garnish with black olives and shredded basil leaves. Serve the turkey with a fresh tomato and onion salad.

Fruity Duck Stir-fry

The pineapple and plum sauce add a sweetness and fruity flavour to this colourful recipe, which blend well with the duck.

NUTRITIONAL INFORMATION

Calories 241	Sugars 7g	
Protein 26g	Fat 8g	
Carbohydrate ...16g	Saturates 2g	

5 mins   25 mins

SERVES 4

INGREDIENTS

4 duck breasts

1 tsp Chinese five-spice powder

1 tbsp cornflour

1 tbsp chilli oil

225 g/8 oz pearl onions, peeled

2 garlic cloves, crushed

100 g/3½ oz baby corn cobs

175 g/6 oz canned pineapple chunks

6 spring onions, sliced

100 g/3½ oz beansprouts

2 tbsp plum sauce

1 Remove any skin from the duck breasts. Cut the duck into thin slices.

2 Mix the Chinese five-spice powder and the cornflour in a bowl. Toss the duck in the mixture until well coated.

3 Heat the oil in a preheated wok. Cook the duck for 10 minutes or until just beginning to go crisp around the edges. Remove from the wok and set aside.

4 Add the onions and garlic to the wok and cook for 5 minutes or until softened. Add the baby corn cobs and cook for another 5 minutes. Add the pineapple, spring onions and beansprouts and cook for 3–4 minutes. Stir in the plum sauce.

5 Return the cooked duck to the wok and toss until well mixed. Transfer to warm serving dishes and serve hot.

COOK'S TIP

Buy pineapple chunks in natural juice rather than syrup for a fresher flavour. If you can only obtain pineapple in syrup, rinse it in cold water and drain thoroughly before using.

Stir-Fried Beef & Beans

In this recipe the green of the beans complements the dark colour of the beef, and everything is served in a rich sauce.

NUTRITIONAL INFORMATION

Calories 381   Sugars 3g
Protein . . . . .25g   Fat 27g
Carbohydrate . . .10g   Saturates 8g

35 mins   15 mins

SERVES 4

I N G R E D I E N T S

450 g/1 lb beef fillet steak or rump steak, cut into 2.5-cm/1-inch pieces

M A R I N A D E

2 tsp cornflour

2 tbsp dark soy sauce

2 tsp ground nut oil

S A U C E

2 tbsp vegetable oil

3 garlic cloves, crushed

1 small onion, cut into 8 pieces

225 g/8 oz thin French beans, halved

25 g/1 oz unsalted cashew nuts

25 g/1 oz canned bamboo shoots, drained

2 tsp dark soy sauce

2 tsp Chinese rice wine or dry sherry

125 ml/4 fl oz beef stock

2 tsp cornflour

4 tsp water

salt and pepper

1 To make the marinade, mix together thoroughly the cornflour, soy sauce and ground nut oil.

2 Place the steak in a shallow glass bowl. Pour the marinade over the steak, turn to coat thoroughly, cover, and marinate in the refrigerator for at least 30 minutes – the longer the better.

3 To make the sauce, heat the oil in a preheated wok. Add the garlic, onion, French beans, cashew nuts, and bamboo shoots, and cook for 2–3 minutes.

4 Remove the steak from the marinade, drain, add to the wok and cook for 3–4 minutes.

5 Mix together the soy sauce, Chinese rice wine or sherry, and beef stock. Blend the cornflour with the water and stir into the soy sauce mixture, mixing everything well to combine.

6 Stir the mixture into the wok and bring the sauce to the boil, stirring until thickened and clear. Lower the heat and simmer for 2–3 minutes. Season to taste and serve immediately.

Lamb Couscous

Couscous is a North African speciality. It is usually accompanied by a spicy mixture of meat or sausage with fruit, which adds a note of luxury.

NUTRITIONAL INFORMATION

Calories . . . . . . .647 Sugars 22g
Protein . . . . .41g Fat 21g
Carbohydrate . . .79g Saturates 6g

 20 mins   20 mins

SERVES 4

I N G R E D I E N T S

2 tbsp olive oil

500 g/1 lb 2 oz lean lamb fillet, thinly sliced

2 onions, sliced

2 garlic cloves, chopped

1 stick of cinnamon

1 tsp ground ginger

1 tsp paprika

½ tsp chilli powder

600 ml/1 pint hot chicken stock

3 carrots, thinly sliced

2 turnips, halved and sliced

400 g/14 oz canned chopped tomatoes

2 tbsp raisins

425 g/15 oz canned chickpeas, drained and rinsed

3 courgettes, sliced

125 g/4½ oz fresh dates, halved and stoned, or 125 g/4½ oz dried apricots

300 g/10½ oz couscous

600 ml/1 pint boiling water

salt

1 Heat the oil in a frying pan and cook the lamb briskly for 3 minutes until browned. Remove from the pan with a slotted spoon and set aside.

2 Add the onions to the pan and cook, stirring constantly, until soft. Add the garlic and spices and cook for 1 minute.

3 Add the chicken stock, carrots, turnips, tomatoes, raisins, chickpeas and lamb, and salt to taste. Cover, bring to the boil, and simmer for 12 minutes.

4 Add the courgettes and the dates. Cover again and cook for 8 minutes.

5 Meanwhile, put the couscous in a bowl with 1 teaspoon of salt and pour the boiling water over it. Let it soak for 5 minutes, then fluff it with a fork.

6 To serve, pile the couscous on to a warmed serving platter and make a hollow in the centre. Put the meat and vegetables in the hollow, and pour some of the sauce over them. Serve the rest of the sauce separately.

Minty Lamb Kebabs

These spicy lamb kebabs go well with the cool cucumber and yogurt dip. In the summer you can barbecue the kebabs outside.

NUTRITIONAL INFORMATION

Calories 295	Sugars 4g
Protein 29g	Fat 18g
Carbohydrate 4g	Saturates 9g

5 mins   20 mins

SERVES 4

INGREDIENTS

2 tsp coriander seeds

2 tsp cumin seeds

3 cloves

3 green cardamom pods

6 black peppercorns

1-cm/½-inch piece root ginger

2 garlic cloves

2 tbsp chopped fresh mint

1 small onion, chopped

400 g/14 oz minced lamb

½ tsp salt

sprigs of fresh mint, to garnish

lime slices, to serve

DIP

150 ml/5 fl oz low-fat natural yogurt

2 tbsp chopped fresh mint

7.5-cm/3-inch piece of cucumber, grated

1 tsp mango chutney

1 Heat a frying pan and then dry-fry the coriander seeds, cumin seeds, cloves, cardamom pods and peppercorns until they turn a shade darker and release a roasted aroma.

2 Grind the spices in a coffee grinder, spice mill, or pestle and mortar.

3 Put the ginger and garlic into a food processor or blender and process to a purée. Add the ground spices, and the mint, onion, lamb and salt and process until finely chopped. Alternatively, finely chop the garlic and ginger and mix with the ground spices and remaining kebab ingredients.

4 Mould the kebab mixture into small sausage shapes on 4 kebab skewers.

Cook under a preheated hot grill for about 10–15 minutes, turning occasionally.

5 To make the dip, mix together the yogurt, fresh mint, cucumber and mango chutney.

6 Garnish the kebabs with sprigs of fresh mint and serve with lime slices and the dip.

Pork with Fennel & Aniseed

In this dish, lean pork chops, stuffed with an aniseed and orange filling, are pan-cooked with fennel in an aniseed-flavoured sweet sauce.

NUTRITIONAL INFORMATION

Calories 298   Sugars 10g
Protein . . . . .30g   Fat 10g
Carbohydrate . . .18g   Saturates 3g

🦀 🦀 🦀

🍳 20 mins   🕐 35 mins

SERVES 4

INGREDIENTS

4 lean pork chops, 125 g/4½ oz each

60 g/2¼ oz brown rice, cooked

1 tsp orange rind, grated

4 spring onions, trimmed and finely chopped

½ tsp aniseed

1 tbsp olive oil

1 bulb fennel, trimmed and thinly sliced

450 ml/16 fl oz unsweetened orange juice

1 tbsp cornflour

2 tbsp Pernod

salt and pepper

fennel fronds, to garnish

cooked vegetables, to serve

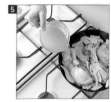

1 Trim away any excess fat from the pork chops. Using a small, sharp knife, make a slit in the centre of each chop to create a pocket.

2 Mix the rice, grated orange rind, chopped spring onions, seasoning and aniseed together in a bowl.

3 Push the rice mixture into the pocket of each chop, then press together gently to seal.

4 Heat the oil in a frying pan and cook the pork chops on each side for 2–3 minutes until lightly browned.

5 Add the sliced fennel and the orange juice to the pan, bring to the boil, and simmer for 15–20 minutes until the meat is tender and cooked through. Remove the pork and fennel with a slotted spoon and transfer to a serving plate.

6 Blend the cornflour and Pernod together in a small bowl. Add the cornflour mixture to the pan and stir into the pan juices. Cook for 2–3 minutes, stirring, until the sauce thickens.

7 Pour the Pernod sauce over the pork chops, garnish with fennel fronds, and serve with a selection of freshly cooked vegetables.

Fruity Pork Skewers

Prunes and apricots bring colour and flavour to these tasty pork kebabs. They are delicious eaten straight off the barbecue.

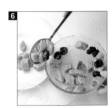

NUTRITIONAL INFORMATION

Calories 205	Sugars 8g
Protein 21g	Fat 10g
Carbohydrate 8g	Saturates 3g

1¼ hrs   15 mins

SERVES 4

I N G R E D I E N T S

4 boneless, lean pork loin steaks

8 ready-to-eat prunes

8 ready-to-eat dried apricots

4 bay leaves

slices of orange and lemon, to garnish

M A R I N A D E

4 tbsp orange juice

2 tbsp olive oil

1 tsp ground bay leaves

salt and pepper

1 Trim the visible fat from the pork and then cut the meat into even-sized chunks.

2 Place the pork chunks in a shallow, non-metallic dish and then add the prunes and apricots.

3 To make the marinade, put the orange juice, oil and bay leaves in a bowl and mix together. Season to taste with salt and pepper.

4 Pour the marinade over the pork and fruit and toss until well coated. Cover and marinate in the refrigerator for at least 1 hour or preferably overnight.

5 Soak 4 wooden skewers in cold water to prevent them catching alight on the barbecue.

6 Using a slotted spoon, lift the pork and fruit from the marinade and reserve the marinade for basting. Thread the pork, fruit and bay leaves alternately on to the skewers.

7 Barbecue the skewers on an oiled rack over medium hot coals for 10–15 minutes, turning and basting frequently with the reserved marinade, or until the pork is cooked through.

8 Transfer the pork and fruit skewers to warm serving plates. Garnish with slices of orange and lemon and serve hot.

Brown Bread Ice Cream

Although it sounds unusual, this yogurt-based recipe is delicious.
It contains no cream and is ideal for a low-fat diet.

NUTRITIONAL INFORMATION

Calories ....264 Sugars 25g
Protein ....12g Fat 6g
Carbohydrate ...43g Saturates 1g

2¼ hrs   5 mins

SERVES 4

INGREDIENTS

175 g/6 oz fresh wholemeal breadcrumbs

25 g/1 oz walnuts, finely chopped

4 tbsp caster sugar

½ tsp ground nutmeg

1 tsp finely grated orange zest

450 ml/16 fl oz low-fat natural yogurt

2 large egg whites

TO DECORATE

walnut halves

orange slices

fresh mint

1 Preheat the grill to medium. Mix together the breadcrumbs walnuts, and sugar and spread over a sheet of foil in the grill pan.

2 Grill the breadcrumb mixture, stirring frequently, for 5 minutes, until crisp and evenly browned (take care that the sugar does not burn). Remove from the heat and leave to cool.

3 When cool, transfer to a mixing bowl and mix in the nutmeg, orange zest and yogurt. In another bowl, whisk the egg whites until stiff. Gently fold into the breadcrumb mixture, using a metal spoon.

4 Spoon the mixture into 4 small moulds, smooth over the tops, and freeze for 1½–2 hours until firm.

5 To serve, hold the bases of the moulds in hot water for a few seconds, then immediately turn the ice cream out on to serving plates.

6 Serve at once, decorated with the walnuts, oranges and fresh mint.

COOK'S TIP

If you do not have small moulds, use ramekins or teacups or, if you prefer, use one large bowl. Alternatively, spoon the mixture into a large, freezerproof container to freeze and serve the ice cream in scoops.

Sweet Carrot Halva

This nutritious dessert is bursting with spices, nuts and raisins. The nutritional information does not include serving with yogurt.

NUTRITIONAL INFORMATION

Calories 284   Sugars 33g
Protein ....7g   Fat 14g
Carbohydrate ...34g   Saturates 3g

🧊 10 mins   🕐 55 mins

SERVES 6

INGREDIENTS

750 g/1 lb 10 oz carrots, grated

700 ml/1¼ pints milk

1 cinnamon stick or piece of cassia
  bark (optional)

4 tbsp ghee or vegetable oil

5 tbsp granulated sugar

25 g/1 oz unsalted pistachio nuts, chopped

4 tbsp blanched almonds, flaked
  or chopped

60 g/2¼ oz seedless raisins

8 cardamom pods, split and seeds removed
  and crushed

sprigs of fresh mint, to decorate

thick natural yogurt, to serve

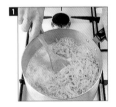 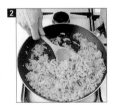 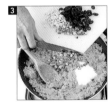

1 Put the grated carrots, milk, and cinnamon or cassia, if using, into a large, heavy saucepan and bring to the boil. Reduce the heat to very low and simmer, uncovered, for 35–40 minutes or until the mixture is thick (with no milk remaining.) Stir the mixture frequently during cooking to prevent it sticking.

2 Remove and discard the cinnamon or cassia. Heat the ghee or oil in a non-stick frying pan, add the carrot mixture, and stir-fry over a medium heat for about 5 minutes or until the carrots take on a glossy sheen.

3 Add the sugar, pistachio nuts, almonds, raisins and crushed cardamom seeds, mix thoroughly, and continue stir-frying for another 3–4 minutes. Serve warm or cold with thick natural yogurt, garnished with sprigs of fresh mint.

COOK'S TIP

The quickest and easiest way to grate this quantity of carrots is by using a food processor fitted with the appropriate blade.

Aromatic Fruit Salad

The fruits in this salad are arranged attractively on serving plates with a spicy syrup spooned over them.

NUTRITIONAL INFORMATION

Calories 125   Sugars 29g
Protein . . . . .3g   Fat 1g
Carbohydrate . . .29g   Saturates 0.2g

 25 mins   5 mins

SERVES 6

I N G R E D I E N T S

½ honeydew melon

large wedge of watermelon

2 ripe guavas

3 ripe nectarines

about 18 strawberries

a little toasted shredded coconut,
    for sprinkling

sprigs of mint or rose petals, to decorate

strained low-fat Greek yogurt, to serve

S Y R U P

3½ tbsp granulated sugar

150 ml/5 fl oz water

1 cinnamon stick or large piece of
    cassia bark

4 cardamom pods, crushed

1 clove

juice of 1 orange

juice of 1 lime

1 To make the syrup, put the sugar, water, cinnamon, cardamom pods and clove into a saucepan and bring to the boil, stirring to dissolve the sugar. Simmer for 2 minutes then remove from the heat.

2 Add the orange juice and lime juice to the syrup. Leave to cool and infuse while preparing the fruits.

3 Peel and remove the seeds from the honeydew melon and watermelon and cut the flesh into neat slices.

4 Cut the guavas in half, scoop out the seeds, then peel carefully and slice the flesh neatly.

5 Cut the nectarines into slices and hull and slice the strawberries.

6 Arrange the slices of fruit attractively on 6 serving plates.

7 Strain the prepared cooled syrup and spoon over the sliced fruits.

8 Sprinkle the fruit salad with a little toasted coconut. Decorate each serving with sprigs of mint or rose petals and serve with yogurt.

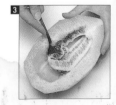